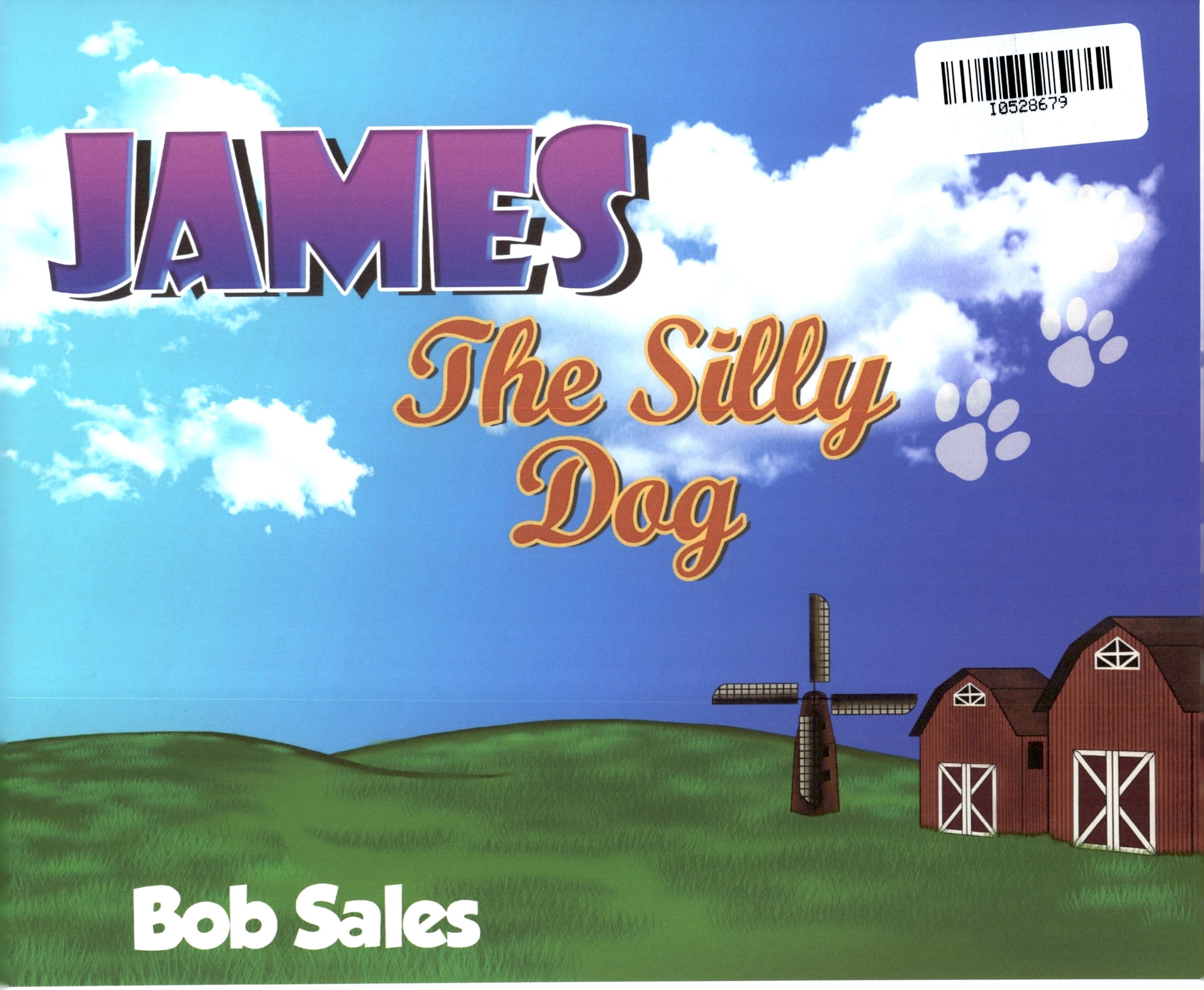

JAMES

The Silly Dog

Bob Sales

Published in the United States of America

ISBN 978-1-962110-92-1 (SC)
ISBN 978-1-963379-40-2 (HC)

Bob Sales Publishing
222 West 6th Street
Suite 400, San Pedro, CA, 90731
www.stellarliterary.com

Order Information and Rights Permission:

Quantity sales. Special discounts might be available on quantity purchases by corporations, associations, and others. For details, contact the publisher at the address above.

For Book Rights Adaptation and other Rights Permission.
Call us at toll-free 1-888-945-8513 or send us an email at admin@stellarliterary.com.

To Mom and Dad.

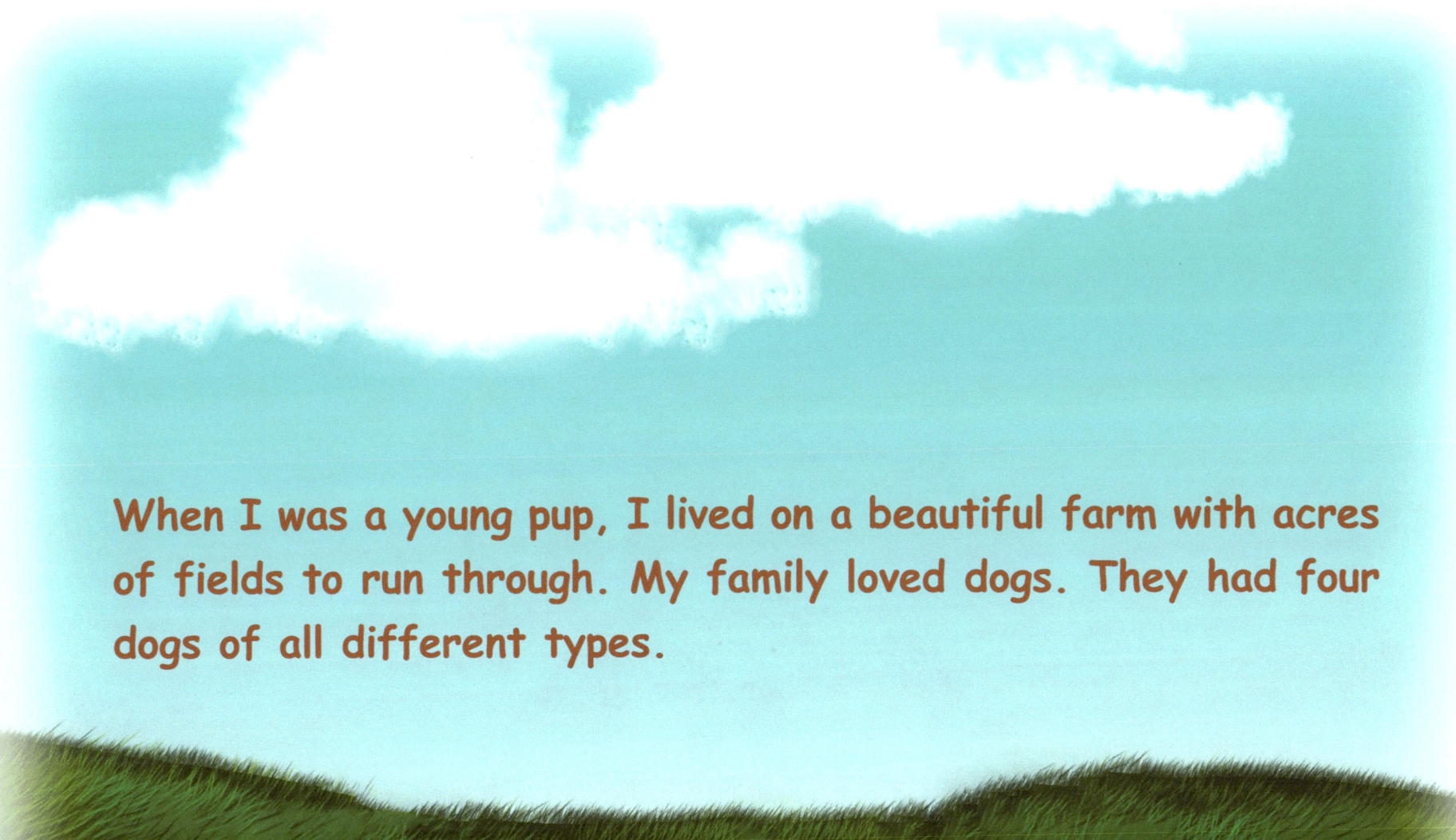

When I was a young pup, I lived on a beautiful farm with acres of fields to run through. My family loved dogs. They had four dogs of all different types.

Snickers, with tons of energy, Biscuit, the tiniest yet toughest dog you ever saw, and Sammy, a dog with big floppy ears. The fourth dog is me, James.

The four of us loved to run around, play, take naps and eat.

But I was the silliest.

I loved to chase birds and squirrels in the field. I don't think they wanted to play with me.

My owners tried to play catch with me, but I never wanted to give the ball back.

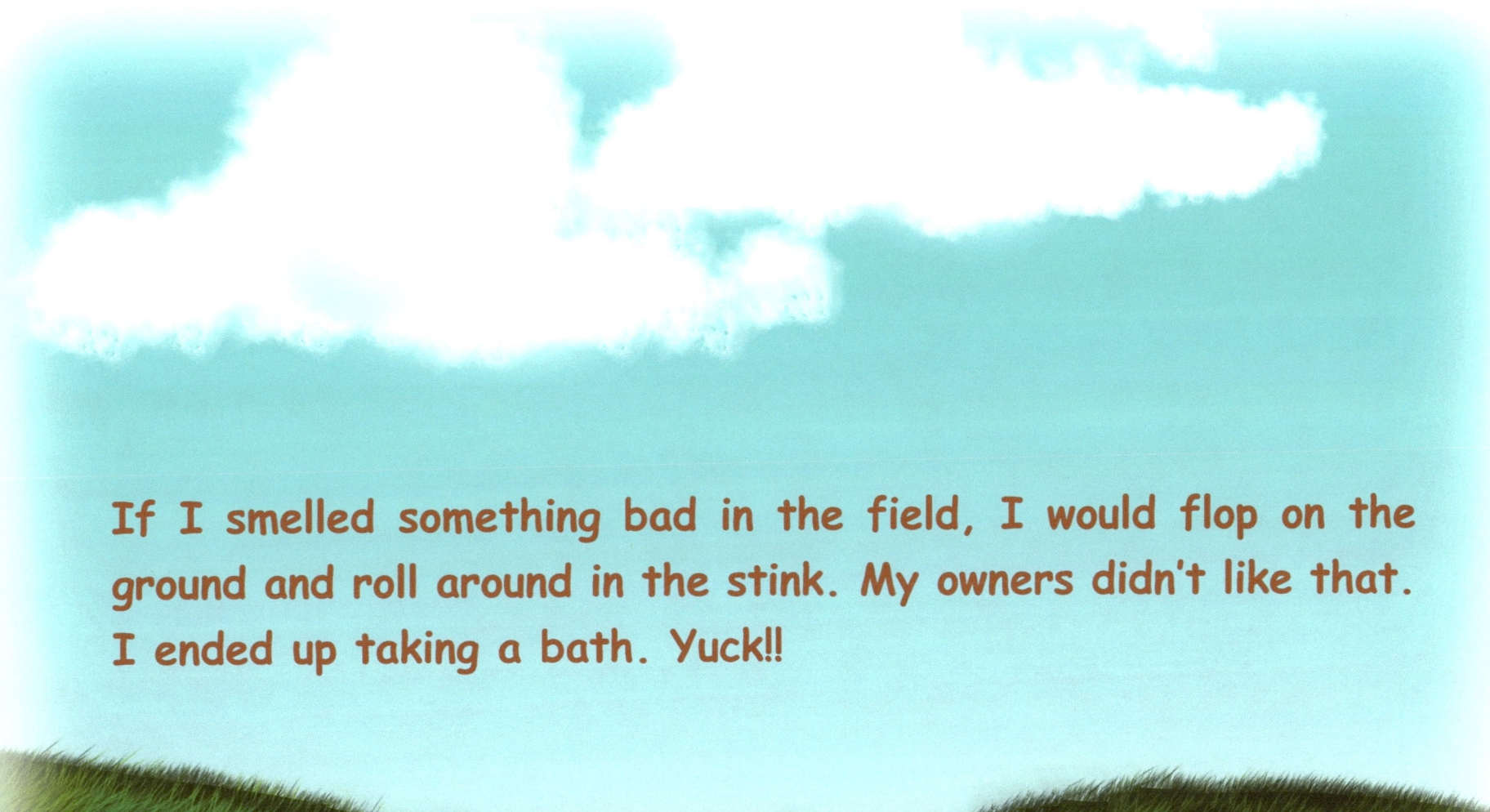

If I smelled something bad in the field, I would flop on the ground and roll around in the stink. My owners didn't like that. I ended up taking a bath. Yuck!!

Another time, a relative was staying in the house and she was mean. She would yell at us, and hit us on the nose with a newspaper when my family wasn't looking. When she was asleep, I went into her room and pooped in her shoes. Thankfully, she never came back.

During meal times, we were all silly. We would try to eat food off the table, or out of the children's hands. This would make the family so mad that we would get sent out to the yucky barn the rest of the night.

One day the family invited friends over for a party. One of the friends brought a wise old Great Dane named Shepherd. Shepherd was so much fun. He liked to play and chase and run.

After all of the playing we went inside to search for food. There was plenty of food. There were roast beef sandwiches, pudding, sweet cakes, and my favorite, cheese. We started to make our way over to the table to try to steal some food when Shepard said, "If you take the food, you will get into trouble and not receive any blessings."

Totally ignoring the Great Dane, Snickers with the big eyes said, "I gotta have that food." He quickly jumped up on the couch and grabbed a sandwich off a television tray. As soon as Snickers took the sandwich, the family immediately sent him out to the barn, with no food.

Small little Biscuit said, "Shepherd, I agree with you, I am not going to take any food." She even went around telling Sammy and me not to steal the food. But, as soon as she said this, a little girl sat down on the floor with some fried chicken that looked oh so tasty. Acting quickly, Biscuit chomped the chicken leg and ran off. She did not get far before the chicken leg was taken from her, and she was sent out to the barn with the taste of the chicken still in her mouth.

Sammy, with his big floppy ears, also agreed with Shepherd. He did not want to steal human food. But after a while, Sammy started to complain about how long it had been since he had eaten, and about how good the chocolate cake smelled. "Woe is me," he said, "If only I could have a small taste." Unable to take it any longer, Sammy stretched his neck out and started licking the chocolate cake on the table. After two licks poor Sammy was sent to the barn to join Snickers and Biscuit. My three friends did not get any food that evening.

Even though I was the silliest, I listened to everything Shepherd said. I knew in my heart he was right.

I was never sent out to the barn that night. My owners even let me eat a plate of food with roast beef, chicken and my favorite, a little cheese.

Even though I am an old dog now, I still remember that all who follow the Good Shepherd will receive many blessings.

Although, I still like to be a little silly. "Want to go for a roll in something stinky?"

www.ingramcontent.com/pod-product-compliance
Lightning Source LLC
Chambersburg PA
CBHW040814120626

46547CB00004B/543